Storyland

Keith Dunlap

Hip Pocket Press Mission Statement

It is our belief that the arts are the embodiment of the soul of a culture, that the promotion of writers and artists is essential if our current culture, with its emphasis on television and provocative outcomes, is to have a chance to develop that inner voice and ear that express and listen to beauty. Toward that end, Hip Pocket Press will continue to search out and discover poets and writers whose voices can give us a clearer understanding of ourselves and of the culture which defines us.

Other Books from Hip Pocket Press

You Notice the Body: Gail Rudd Entrekin (poetry)
Terrain: Dan Bellm, Molly Fisk, Forrest Hamer (poetry)
A Common Ancestor: Marilee Richards (poetry)
Sierra Songs & Descants: Poetry & Prose of the Sierra: Gail Rudd Entrekin, Ed.
Truth Be Told: Tom Farber (epigrams)
Songs for a Teenage Nomad: Kim Culbertson (young adult fiction)
Yuba Flows: Kirsten Casey, Gary Cooke, Cheryl Dumesnil, Judy Halebsky, Iven Lourie & Scott Young; Gail Rudd Entrekin, Ed. (poetry)
The More Difficult Beauty: Molly Fisk (poetry)
Ex Vivo (Out of the Living Body): Kirsten Casey (poetry)
Even That Indigo: John Smith (poetry)
The Berkeley Poets Cooperative: A History of the Times: Charles Entrekin, Ed. (essays)
Jester: Grace Marie Grafton (poetry)
The Occasionist: Curt Anderson (poetry)

Web Publications

Canary, a Literary Journal of the Environmental Crisis:
   hippocketpress.org/canary
Sisyphus, Essays on Language, Culture & the Arts:
   hippocketpress.org/Sisyphus

Storyland

Keith Dunlap

HPP
HIP POCKET PRESS

Orinda, California
2016

Published by Hip Pocket Press
5 Del Mar Court
Orinda, CA 94563
www.hippocketpress.org

This edition was produced for on-demand distribution by lightningsource.com for Hip Pocket Press.

Typesetting: Wordsworth (wordsworthofmarin.com)
Cover art & design: Kris Woolsey
Author photo: Kris Woolsey

Copyright © 2016 by Keith Dunlap

No part of this book may be reproduced or transmitted in any form or by any means, graphic, electronic or mechanical, including photocopying, recording, taping or by any information storage or retrieval system, without permission in writing from the publisher.

Printed in the United States of America.

ISBN: 0-917658-47-7
ISBN 13: 978-0-917658-47-1

To Emily Case Guernsey, my grandmother, who taught me how to read, to drink tea, and to be part of a conversation.

Acknowledgments

Versions of these poems have been published in the following journals, as indicated:

"Loggerheads" in *Apeiron Review*
"The Last Poem I'll Ever Write" in *Barnwood*
"Sunday Puzzle" in *Borderlands: Texas Poetry Review*
"Dante Gabriel Rosetti to Elizabeth," "The Abandoned Psychiatric Hospital," and "The Former Slaughterhouse at Villa Epecuén" in *The Café Review*
"Storyland" in *The Cape Rock*
"Melting Faster" and "In Memoriam" in *The Carolina Quarterly*
"Reading Greek Tragedy" in *The Common Online*
"The Ring" in *The Comstock Review*
"The Old Man in the Mirror" and "1922 Kodachrome Test Footage" in *Concho River Review*
"A Depressed Man Experiences Joy" in *The Cossack Review*
"The Invitation" in *Eclipse*
"On Looking for my Friend and Not Finding Him," in *Falling Star*
"The Night J.R. Ewing Drove Keith Moon to Rehab" in *floor_plan_journal*
"Lines Written at the Northampton Lunatic Asylum" in *Georgetown Review*
"Close Enough," "The Dalai Lama on the Treadmill," "The Oil Lamp," "Superman," and "Watching an Eighty-Four-Year-Old Man on a Bike Get Hit by a Car in the Whole Foods Parking Lot" in *The Hamilton Stone Review*
"The Final Push" in *The Jabberwock Review*
"The Dying Slaves" in *The Meadow*
"The Escapist" in *Ninth Letter*
"The Longest Day of the Year" in *Poet Lore*
"Into the Mystic" in *Poetry Quarterly*
"La Chevy Nova" in *Qua*
"Ryan's Daughter" in *Slipstream*
"Harry Shunk" in *Sou'wester*
"Music Unheard" in *Star 82*
"Full of Woe" in *Talking River Review*
"The Turk" in *Tipton Poetry Journal*
"Maybe Not the Same Experience," "Prisoners of Love," and "The Riptide" in *Triggerfish Critical Review*
"Ubi Mater Est" in *The Tulane Review*.

Contents

Headlights   1

Levitation of Frogs   2

The Perfume Concert   3

Vietnam   4

Vengeance Is Mine   5

In Memoriam   6

Melting Faster   7

Blonde Wig   8

The Dying Slaves   9

Maybe Not the Same Experience   11

The Oil Lamp   12

Storyland   13

Coon Dog Graveyard   15

Ryan's Daughter   16

Harry Shunk   17

The Dalai Lama on the Treadmill   18

Mapping the Invisible Eye   19

Full of Woe   20

1922 Kodachrome Test Footage   21

All That Jazz   22

The Turk   23

The Escapist   24

Reading Greek Tragedy   26

Watching an Eighty-Four-Year-Old Man on a Bike Get Hit by a Car in the Whole Foods Parking Lot   28

The Departure Lounge   29

The Night J.R. Ewing Drove Keith Moon to Rehab   30

Sunday Puzzle   31

The Ring   32

Lines Written at the Northampton General Lunatic Asylum   34

Prisoners of Love   35

Interior Design   36

Into the Mystic   37

The Invitation (after Carl Dennis)   38

Sideshow   43

The Last Poem I'll Ever Write   44

The Abandoned Psychiatric Hospital   45

The Final Push   46

Close Enough   47

The Angels at the Party   48

Lucky Strikes   49

At the Pompeii Gift Shop   50

La Chevy Nova   51

The Longest Day of the Year   52

Superman   53

McDonald's Lobster Roll   54

A Depressed Man Experiences Joy   55

The Ballerina on the Golden Bicycle   56

The Stuff That Flies Around   58

Decomposing Nicely   59

Dante Gabriel Rosetti to Elizabeth   60

The Former Slaughterhouse at Villa Epecuén   61

House of Cards   62

The Unbearable Lightness of Being Fifteen   63

On Looking for my Friend and Not Finding Him   64

Loggerheads   65

Grace   66

Bright Star   67

Music Unheard   68

The Riptide   69

The Eclogues   70

Walking Through my Hometown Just Before Winter   72

Ubi Mater Est   73

The Normal Rhythmic Clenching of the Heart   74

The Old Man in the Mirror   75

Headlights

The rain so unrelenting that the rain
and the sound of rain are one pragmatic roaring,
a cataract through which the logging truck
ahead of us laboriously climbs:
on one side, the blur of an angry forest
crowding as close as it can,
like a mob pressed against a chain-link fence
to watch us slowly die;
on the other side, we can only guess
that the precipitous decline is a bottomless well
into which our car could be tossed like a coin.
So why then does my husband persist
in trying to pass the lumbering truck,
as if each indivisible moment is a torture
from which he must immediately escape,
pulling out in suicidal hope
that nothing is coming our way?

Levitation of Frogs

stuff happens
in the imagination
the table is a rectangle
on the table is a pan
in the water in the pan
a gray green frog
the weakest force
charged through
with electromagnetism
can hold the frog
as lightly as a prayer
hovering uncertainly
but quite content
in the moist midair
unblinking yellow glassine eyes
staring at the scientist
who put it there

The Perfume Concert

(to Ian Bang)

There is no instrument, no stage,
just two young women in heavy make-up
standing next to electric fans
and two boxes of fabric
soaked in perfume so that
the smell of roses fills the room.
The two young women wave the linens
in the air.

      No point in trying
to make the audience understand;
no point in trying to outlast
the impatient shuffling of hipster shoes
or the derisive commentary
as the crowd spills onto the street
after the sixteen-minute show.
It doesn't matter what we know;
no point in trying to connect
the various sensations of displeasure
that move us from one fugitive spot to the next.

Vietnam

The bleating of a train at the crossing
several neighborhoods away reminds me of the time
in 1967 when my little brother and I
lay across the back seat of the Dodge Dart
while our father, with his army tan,
his white v-neck tee-shirt and his madras shorts,
sat on the hood, smoking Lucky Strikes,
and waited for the train to pass.
He was driving us across the border
to stay with some friends of the family
at their lakeside home. The cattails
along the side of the road
swayed like prairie grass. The air was thick
with mosquitoes and something else—
indecision perhaps. As if,
as one empty boxcar after another trundled past,
we could sense his hesitation; as if
we could hear him wonder
whether it was worth it to keep going,
or whether we should just turn back.

Vengeance Is Mine

I want the twilight to last:
the clouds underlit by darkening night,
a car door slamming across the street,
the dull thud, like a body on concrete,
the over-worked ignition
coughing into a tubercular thrumming,
the demented refrain rewired
in my brain, the neighbor's wife
screaming at the fleeing car,
"You can keep your fucking life."

In Memoriam

If time had an end,
I would stay with you when it came.
I would hold your stubborn head,
as the last lonely thought of it remained.
I would read again to you the letter
that you wrote so long ago,
when you were a student in Paris
and I was your faithless friend,
the letter in which you described
your small, sun-filled apartment
and the noise the American couple made
arguing in the street below;
so that when the end came,
we would know exactly where we had been,
exactly where we had started,
and exactly where we were then.
We could read the last part together
in the minuscule, painstaking letters
of your handwriting at the bottom of the page,
where you had carefully written,
"Is this how everything ends?"

Melting Faster

The last ten minutes are a blur I cannot shed
the feeling I'm supposed to say something
that thirty-five thousand years of preparation
that thirty-five thousand years of one good idea
holding down another and slitting its throat
deserves some memoration,
but as I fumble in the pocket of my coat, fingering
my keys, a cough drop, and a forgotten note,
I cannot help but think that everything I've read,
everything I've done, thought, or said is undone;
all because the slender-waisted girl who held the door,
held the door for me and said,
"The dead don't know they're dead."

Blonde Wig

I can't say I know for certain that
something which happened so long ago—staggering
through Chinatown in a blonde wig on Halloween,
after coming out of a blackout—ever really happened.
And even then the only thing I remembered was
a somewhat too insistent exclamation by
a Norwegian engineering student who said,
"You make a very beautiful woman," and grabbed
my sleeve as if to stop me from falling and push me down
at the same time. I awoke on my hands and knees,
clutching the tacky trash-strewn pavement underneath the FDR,
not sure of where I was or how to find my way
out of the dark forest of rust-blackened girders that held
the rattling thunderous highway overhead. The frightened taxis fled
me waving my blousy arms, desperate, nervous of the Filipino
laborers not far off who wrangled an American Airlines
shipping container off a truck and onto the warehouse bay.
They did not mind my being there.
They did not mind my leaving, and, to this day,
I have no recollection of how I finally made it home.

The Dying Slaves

I.

When the doctor told me about the lump I did not go
to greet my wife and child with the morbid news, but instead
I bought a ticket at the Greyhound station on Saint John Street
to New York. Once there I had enough left for
a hot dog and a pack of cigarettes. I ate my lunch
and smoked away the day on the steps of the Museum,
only heading inside when it was close to closing time,
walking quietly against the tide of fleeing crowds, straight for
antiquities, following the same path I had been following
since I was eighteen, straight to the Roman copy of the Dying Slave,
attributed to Kallicles, but it wasn't there, and then
I remembered that it never was, that it was on display in the Capitoline,
and sculpted, in fact, by Michelangelo,
and I laughed at all my foolishness, every precious bit of it,
until a nervous guard politely reminded me that it was time to go.

II.

There's a picture of me, my little brother, and my friend,
outside a topless bar in Buffalo in late July.
I can easily recollect how hot it was, how high we were,
how funny it all seemed, when we all lifted our shirts to our chins,
like three dying slaves caught by the camera's flash in the only moment that lasts:
that is, the moment that is both adolescent and contrived,
fleshy, marbled, unselfconscious, a dream of acute forgetfulness.

III.

I have an ancient postcard in black and white, a reproduction
of the Dying Slave, which I have kept with me all these years.
Its borders have yellowed and its matte surface has rubbed thin.
His head turned back in ecstasy, his hands almost to his chin,
he seems more godlike than any god, as if
even cold stone death cannot rob him of his pagan pleasure,
and all the religions that created him can only marvel at his mortality.

Maybe Not the Same Experience

But something happened to me at the same time,
far away. My radio tuned to the same station
which broadcast the Gregorian chant.
The medieval polyphony consoled me,
instructed me as would a passage of religious
philosophy, after I had learned about the death
of an old college friend, the news
delivered in an email from a mutual acquaintance,
the sort who takes unconscious pleasure
from relaying such distressing accidents,
as if the rest of us needed to be taught a lesson,
to have our confidence humbled and our joys delayed.
For you, it was the spirit-destroying daily stress,
momentarily allayed by the cadent repetition,
recorded in the echoing cave of a Gothic cathedral,
as if, as you neatly folded sandwiches into plastic bags
for the kids, each endless annoying morning task
were also a sacred duty. We stopped.
And listened. The music asked
for quiet. And reverential repose.

The Oil Lamp

The Coleman lantern inside my tent,
(which I know you're not supposed to do,)
gives me light enough to read my book,
but not enough to banish the darkness completely.

My tent is one of many at this site:
one of many tents and self-extinguishing fires
scattered around the campground,
above which stars swim like silver fish, like Latin sounds.

I am alone beneath the narrow fitting flaps,
which makes no sense to me at all
because I'm married and have a daughter
and wouldn't go camping without them.

Yet here I am and reading *The Art of Love*
by Publius Ovidius Naso,
a paperback translation of the poem
with the Latin on the facing page.

I am reading the English text—although
once I could have read the Latin too.
Now, however, the couplets are like shadowy fish
in a stream. I can't grab them. They shimmy away,

then loiter just out of reach. What I know,
or once knew, or perhaps only thought I knew,
is just like that, like someone whispering in a dream:
Cera vadum temptet, rasis infusa tabellis.

Storyland

> "Bring, bring the barley cake—quick as you can, for Mr. Beetle."
> Aristophanes, *The Peace*

I am standing still, watching my daughter
on the merry-go-round at Storyland,
her smile fading in and out, as her aquamarine
one-piece bathing suit flashes brightly by.
She is riding a fantastically pink stallion,
the reins frozen in her hands, but that
doesn't deter her from trying to make the horse rock back and forth,
as if she doesn't quite understand what is moving
and what is stationary. With each revolution
the sounds of the amusement park whir around:
the delighted screams of children,
the frantic mechanical music of the carousel,
and the duller sounds, the anxious shuffling of sneakers on concrete,
and the sort of family fight that is an inevitable tributary
of so much forced cheerfulness, all loitering
beneath the lowering humid and gray but not yet raining sky;
making me slightly melancholy and bewildered too,
as if each time I see my daughter again she's someone new,
or rather someone who never before existed;
as if the old-fashioned ride were a time machine
out of a book, an antique contraption,
that by spinning in one place,
sweeps us all at once into the ordinary summer air
alongside the circling ride, and sets some simple science project
into motion, an experiment in physics to prove
that everything that will ever happen has already taken shape,
and every part of history is just about to be;

so that I suddenly feel an uncertainty not unlike
the time when I myself was four and took an old shoebox
and sealed it shut with string and cellophane tape,
punching holes in the top but not so big
that anyone could tell that there was nothing inside;
and, taking it with me to kindergarten,
convinced my teacher and my class I had a pet
that I didn't have, a rabbit in the box,
which no one was allowed to see.
Who cares now whether this thing is false or true?
Mrs. Pelto, my kindergarten teacher,
during that spring vacation long ago, called our home, in tears,
to confess that my nonexistent rabbit had escaped,
and offered to pay us to replace him; and now,
as if on cue, my daughter swings around the bend,
head down, whispering in the ear of her pink horse,
urging him on, to gallop down the course,
as if she could outpace the other young girls and boys.
And I want to shout, *You can do it, you really can.*
That ridiculous Pegasus will heed your command.
We are not just going in circles or standing in place.
A man will say you're pretty, and he will want to kiss your face,
And you will be pretty, and wishes will fall from the sky
Like drops of rain on a humid summer day at Storyland.
But, as the mawkish recorded music stops short,
and the ride grinds to a halt, my daughter's attention drifts
around the outlines of things as if she is a little dizzy
and doesn't quite understand what is spinning
and what is certain and still, as if she is not quite aware
of what is or is not really there.

Coon Dog Graveyard

Thousands of people visit every year
although the spot is hard to find
as you wind through the hills near Cherokee
until you see a small hand-painted sign
with a red arrow pointing to the Coon Dog Cemetery.
The first headstone was placed in 1937,
chiseled by a whiskey man named Key Underwood
with a hammer and a screwdriver,
marking the grave of Old Troop,
"The best damned dog that ever run these woods."
Coon hunting is a night sport,
the time when old men crowd a fire
and trade the elaborations that keep them all together,
the dogs released at dusk,
from corn patch, hollow, or dry bed.
It takes years to train a whelp to tree a coon,
ignoring armadillos and a forest full of squirrels,
"choppin' steady" so you know he's cornered his quarry.
It's a cliché to say that losing a good hound is like losing an old friend,
but a dog still needs three references to get in,
to join Dr. Doom, Preacher, Squeak, and Lulabelle
on the crest of a shady but otherwise insignificant hill,
where under an arbor in a three-ringed binder,
which serves as a guest book, Mrs. Henrietta Small
from West Lebanon has written in wonder,
"I've never seen anything like it and don't think I ever will."

Ryan's Daughter

When I was ten and my brother eight,
our parents took us to the drive-in to see
Ryan's Daughter. By the time we got there,
the cartoons had already started,
the giant dizzy technicolor madcap
floating above us in disconnected space.
As our massive station wagon slowly
crawled through the shadowy herd of cars,
its wheels crunching the gravel,
we could nonetheless discern the chorus of mechanical voices
hung in the other windows,
all suddenly laughing the insane cackle
of Woody Woodpecker at the same time.
My brother and I wore our pajamas
and had a kind of bed we shared,
the backseat folded down,
and blankets and pillows spread
around. I don't remember much
from the movie, except the scene
when a young British soldier fucks
a beautiful Irish girl
in an endless field of rye,
the soft green and white stalks undulating in the breeze,
as if the world itself were suddenly quiet and tense,
a tremulous surface of leaves,
in which no one else was breathing,
until my mother gave a little gasp,
and asked me to cover my brother's eyes.

Harry Shunk

But man can fly.
Like Yves Klein in *Saut Dans le Vide,*
who threw himself into the air
from the ledge of a second-story window
above a paved and narrow street,
(patched with asphalt and green where
weeds broke through) while another man, Harry Shunk,
took his picture; so that, in the picture, anyway,
he remained for that moment, however long it was,
suspended forever above the passing world. In fact,
the man in the Wellington,
who bicycled by did not see him fall, but
did not see him fly either. Or was he falling
and flying at the same time? *C'est la vie.* It is
this uncertainty that makes the world alive.

The Dalai Lama on the Treadmill

He has been old for a very long time now.
The lenses of his glasses fogged with exertion
sit askew on his weathered happy face.
His mindful breaths come and go, come and go,
as he takes in stride the inclined conveyor. He maintains
a steady, determined pace, just as a linebacker
would, jogging onto the field, after the coach
has given him the play, holding him by the shoulders,
staring him in the eyes and letting him know
that the other team must not score.
The rubber tread slips away beneath his bare feet,
rebounding under each step like a muffled trampoline.
He is going nowhere. Not fast, not standing still exactly,
in the same way that the earth doesn't seem to move,
yet courses around the sun at approximately 107,000 kilometers per hour.

I put the magazine, which has a picture of the Dalai Lama on a treadmill, down,
step outside, cross the damp pavers tinged with algae,
cross the unruly pitch of grass that feeds
into the ravine at the property line,
and sit in my favorite unpainted chair, the one beneath
the silver maple. Alone. Not alone. The wind high overhead
stirs the awestruck trees. The cloudless sky, a northern blue
as shallow as a membrane, seems to stall, as if the spinning world has stopped.
The breeze drops. This moment is sacred too.
The real is real enough. This momentary reflection, which
reanimates every shimmering shaking detail of the day, creates
a magnificent invitation—intricate, haphazard, transitory, eternal, one
which does not advance a theory, does not retreat, but allows
me to be a part of it, to feel the wind, to hear the sound,
to see it bend the tops of the trees.

Mapping the Invisible Eye

Jenny is asleep and the room is dark.
I am on my hands and knees,
searching for shoes before I leave for work.
I am like a drunk who has lost his keys,
feeling around in the baffling pitch,
the ground a sinkhole of fading consciousness.
I had a buddy out on the street
who fell and hit his head.
He couldn't endure the hospital routines—
the waiting and the forms;
more than any diagnosis, he needed to drink some Listerine.
They found him dead behind the Rite Aid store,
an aneurysm having flooded his brain.
Yet here I am twenty years later,
a marriage, a child, and a house,
fumbling around on the floor,
not drunk but like a drunk,
trying not to disturb my wife.

Full of Woe

Last night I heard my daughter laughing in her sleep.
The electronic gurgling through the intercom sounded
strange, yet drew me from the pitch of absolute solitude
and back into the fragile comfort I call my life.

Delight is the wrong word for this, too demanding;
the best I can do is let the silence come when it comes,
let my wife sleep quietly beside me on the bed,
let the bed float as it will on the tide of shadows and false alarms between us.

1922 Kodachrome Test Footage

All the subjects are women
in fashions of the day,
the colors and folds of their clothes
as bold as lipstick shades,
pale powdered skin trembling
in the creamy light,
flickering like Mary Pickford
or Edna St. Vincent Millay.
It makes the studied flirtation
that much more intense,
like jazz age linotypes
delicately animated
into the tinted frames
of a kinescope,
as if for the first time
the person were a work of art
and any given shop girl
a stop-frame Pygmalion
awkwardly coming to life.
No wonder my grandmother,
a flapper when sin was sin,
never found satisfaction
in chain-smoking or her gin,
walking down an urban street
in Paris, New York, or Berlin,
all the women and the men
flush with new invented color,
unfolding like hothouse flowers.

All That Jazz

A junkie with a broken arm
weaves across traffic against the light,
his shirt torn around his ragged neck
like a bandage cut from a larger cloth,
the frame of his bike so badly bent
that the wheels cannot stay his intended course.
He pitches forward and to the side
as if the entire system is about to collapse,
as if he is going to lose his balance,
the wheels fall off, the handlebars break,
the chain slip from the grinding gears,
so that, like some sad comic-book character,
he is suddenly left suspended in midair,
pedaling nothing, steering nowhere.
But it is we in our air-conditioned cars
who give him sway, who slow to a stop
as he makes his way across the busy street
to meet whatever destiny awaits him
on this random corner or the next.
We are the orchestra. He is playing his solo.
And we are in awe until he has finished.

The Turk

> *Each of us learns a difficult thing*
> *That once learned becomes our bane,*
> *Our only consolation that those who do it best*
> *Are also hollowed by their craft and know*
> *There are no magic strings.*

A chess-playing automaton
from the late eighteenth century
tilts his turbaned brow slightly forward,
extends his stiff arms from his fur-trimmed cloak,
and his immobile eyes painted jet
stare from a face as dark as bronze,
which sports a thick sable "Asiatic" moustache.
He is not unexplainable:
a clockwork mechanism fills
the cabinet beneath the table
where the chess board sits,
over which his wooden hands hover,
as if petrified mid-incantation.
He seems to ponder his opponent's move
but does not betray any intent
until suddenly, awkwardly, and without remorse,
his robotic arm
pushes a pawn forward.
It takes less mastery
than one might think
to crouch inside the cabinet
and play a secret game of chess,
to cause the Turk's right hand to act
as if inspired by intelligence—
as if a soul could be replaced
by a whirring clock and springs
and beat a local man from Gridley's pub
who for a few shillings
would put his skill to the test.

The Escapist

at the movies
there was something
I wanted to tell you
but I was distracted
by the silhouette
of the woman
sitting in front of us
the way her hand
covered her mouth
when she laughed
almost as if
she were wearing kid gloves
like it was the fifties
or something
the movie was called
The Escape Artist
it was not a real movie
but a movie I was imagining
while writing a poem
in which a man
gets locked in a safe
and the safe gets thrown
into a river
the safe is airtight
and as it sinks
the man has enough
air to breathe and
plenty of time
to think in the real movie

there was a woman
who wore long white gloves
she was a safecracker
she drove a Vespa
she drove the man
crazy but she
couldn't help him
escape his life
he was doomed
and then I remembered
what it was I wanted
to tell you

Reading Greek Tragedy

The other day as I was searching for a book
to lend a friend who was reading once again
the plays of Aeschylus and Sophocles, I found
a tattered copy of *Reading Greek Tragedy*
by Cambridge professor Simon Goldhill.
And as I was reminiscing through the text,
a letter I had written twenty years ago
fell out between the pages into my hands,
a letter I had written to my puzzled parents
after spending a shortened week with them
at their condominium in Florida.
The letter refers to "the whole wonderful mob,"
which indicates that my sister and my little brother
were there together with their families.
I had always been a mystery to them all:
tall, good-looking, erudite, and yet
incapable of finding a foothold in the world.
And as I re-read the words of this old letter,
the mood of my visit revealed itself to me.
I must have been a "pill" the whole time,
as my acerbic mother would insist,
enough so that I felt it necessary
to make some kind of half-hearted amends.
I was in year one of graduate school
in Classics, reading Ancient Greek,
and Latin history and philosophy
all day, making sure that I was done by ten
so that I could go to my favorite bar, the Marlin,
to drink and smoke the night away with friends.
Each morning I would dutifully start my day
by teaching first-year students Greek at nine,
so I honestly couldn't comprehend
why on earth my advisor might feel the need
to warn me that certain department heads
had some concerns about my drinking.

My mom and I hadn't fought about that, thank god;
instead I had been giving her a hard time
about the decision she had made to shun
my absent older brother and defend
his former wife and his "disputed" child,
his daughter, whom my brother disavowed—
reserving her attention for a girl
she hardly knew, her granddaughter,
at the expense of her troubled oldest son.
The letter didn't spell out any arguments,
and stopped just short of an apology
but asked my mom to put aside her fear.
"It takes my judgment much more seriously
than I take either it or me," it said,
and reminded her of our consanguinity,
and that independence was a quality,
together with dispassion and panache,
nurtured in me by them and only them.
The whole epistle sounded a bit odd.
It didn't fit my recollection of that time,
and didn't fit the image of myself,
which I had since remorsefully preserved:
someone arrogant, defensive, and partially deranged
by alcohol. Instead, there was a studied grace,
a balance and maturity of thought
of which I never gave myself the credit.
And only after reading it the second time
could I discern the Cicero and Seneca in it,
as if the letter had been engendered
and ennobled by a kind of ventriloquism,
as if the words of Socrates and the stately prose
of Roman authors had endowed my mind
for a time with a wisdom alien to me;
the only thing not seeming strange
was that I never sent it.

Watching an Eighty-Four-Year-Old Man on a Bike Get Hit by a Car in the Whole Foods Parking Lot

He fell the way an inappropriate joke falls
on a tense crowd. Everyone too paralyzed
to stop him. He fell the way
the bag of groceries left on top of the station wagon
fell as the driver slammed her brakes:
frozen corn, organic macaroni, canned peas
spilling onto the parking lot like glass beads.
His bike slid awkwardly out beneath him.
And when he landed on the pavement,
like a man suddenly seized with a need for prayer,
there was no sound, no cry of pain,
just the ladder of his parts collapsing.
Yet, as the young woman vaulted from her car,
her beautiful green eyes trembling with disaster,
the flume of her Irish-American hair aflame in the sun
like an emergency flare, he sprang to his feet,
waved, smiled too broadly, and shouted, "I'm okay,"
so that his assailant began to laugh uncontrollably with relief,
laughing and crying at the same time,
rivulets of tears on her freckle-stained cheeks,
as he put his arm around her shoulder to console her.

The Departure Lounge

A woman beats her frantic child curled
on the floor of the ladies' room
at the airport in Birmingham, Alabama,
with the buckle of her unloosed belt,
screaming, "Don't you ever sass me again,
you fucking little whore, you ungrateful bitch,"
herself unloosed in a blind and bitter rage.

I tell her if she doesn't stop, I'm going to call the cops,
but she looks at me as if she doesn't know what I mean.
Staring at me, belt in hand, glaring at me
as if I'm the one who doesn't understand.

It makes me old again and weary,
too old to return home on this flight,
my bones all out of joint on the vinyl chrome-armed couch,
and the earbuds of my iPod
drowning any wisdom or compassion out.
Instead beneath the strains of Joni Mitchell's "Little Green"
a mass of static hisses its secret name,
and as the practiced announcement booms around me,
echoing across the lounge: *Attention passengers.*
We are now boarding people who need assistance
and families with small children, my attention follows
the same sniffling child dragged to the gate without resistance.

The Night J.R. Ewing Drove Keith Moon to Rehab

There was trouble getting in and out of the car.
Hagman drove absentmindedly, forgetting to turn on the lights,
drove at a cautious speed into the Westwood night.
Keith Moon fiddled with the radio but couldn't find a song
that didn't make him want to crawl out of his skin.
"These drummers all suck," he said, chain-smoking Marlboro Reds.
He climbed over the seat and into the back in order to lie down.
He drummed on the leather headrest, made faces, clowned around.
And all this time Larry Hagman kept his eyes fixed on the road.
But when he realized that he had forgotten to turn on the lights,
he flicked them on, so that they carved a path in front of the car,
so that he could clearly see the shoulder on the canyon side,
and, relaxing his grip a little on the steering wheel,
felt that he himself was something greater than the darkness
that he and his passenger had momentarily left behind.

Sunday Puzzle

Just the word *Sunday* in the title
makes me think of her and how she loved
Wallace Stevens, at least his poetry,
and of her sister, the forty-year-old Buddhist,
who read "Sunday Morning" at her memorial service,
and how Philip and I wept into each other's arms,
each of us conscious of how each of us fell short
of her love. What it was for Philip I couldn't say,
but for me it was that day when sick from chemotherapy
she confessed that her dying wish was for us to go away
together and have sex before she was too frail,
and I promised her we would, knowing full well
that it would never come to pass. And then she asked
what I thought happened after death,
and I got all tongue-tied and gave
some lame pseudo-philosophical reply,
when all she wanted me to do was deceive her
when I told the truth and be truthful when I lied.

The Ring

I had been raking leaves for a long time,
looking for my wedding band,
which seemed to fly off my finger
onto the front lawn and disappear.
I bought the ring at a pawn shop downtown,
the one next door to Charlie's Bar and Grill.
It was on display in a glass case,
not far from the handguns.
I bought this ring because it was 18 carat gold.
The purity of the gold gave the ring a red-tinged luster.
It had the motto,
"H.S.J. L.M.J. Forever 1948" inscribed inside.
I thought about those initials a lot,
a young man home from the war,
a woman glad to be off the ranch,
both living in a house paid for by the G.I. Bill.
Money was tight back then.
The ring had to be an extravagance.
I myself paid seventy dollars cash for it,
a little extra, but worth it, after all.

I was just about to give up looking—
it was going to snow soon anyway.
The day had turned cold all of a sudden,
the way it can on a late October afternoon in Montana.
Still, I knew the ring was there, somewhere hidden,
either embedded in the grass
or swept up in the leaves;
to give up was a kind of failure.
But I wasn't wearing gloves,
my fingers were red and numb,
and I could barely hold the rake.

Mount Sentinel, its broad outline
like a woman who has turned her back
against her snoring husband and his half-hearted ways,
didn't care. When it snowed,
it always snowed on the mountain first,
the isolated melting flakes pulling the gray sky down
around its slumbering shoulders.

Lines Written at the Northampton General Lunatic Asylum

(John Clare)

what I do is for me
in a world full of worry
I am a sound
like hazel wood afire

disheveled I wander
in the quickening maze
east of me, winter,
west of me, winter days

I stumble into the world's own chaos

with meaning constructed
from the simple earth's delight

Prisoners of Love

There is no station, only a parking lot
next to an underused laundromat,
where two men sit idly smoking,
waiting for their clothes to dry.
As the bus leaves her behind,
she tightens her grip on the suitcase,
which she stole in El Paso,
trying to appear like someone
who would carry a suitcase full of clothes,
someone also who has many friends,
even in this strange, angry, and dust-blown town.
She has seen it happen—
faces bright with fake surprise
rushing into each other's arms—
because that's what people do.
The movies make this much clear.
In reality, it's hard to imagine
how little anyone cares
whether she has a reason to delay
before she strides into the unforgiving air,
stranded in the seething daylight,
making a show of checking her watch
and a practiced pout of annoyance,
as if her problem were someone else's tardiness,
and not this platform out to nowhere.

Interior Design

Standing near a historiated capital
in the crypt of the Cathedral of Saint-Denis,
a young girl sings just off key
a popular song of the day,
which must at the same time be playing
on the earbuds of her handheld device:
"I'm just a girl and I'm on fire."
Her voice is low in the official silence,
as indistinct and uncertain as a premonition
there in the late medieval martyrium,
the flare of the whispered lyric melting
meekly into the corners of the vault
and the shadow of the melody warming
into a tentative sentimental glow,
as if in the feeble echo of a young girl's voice
in the close and sacral chamber
there is something that is worth it to know.

Into the Mystic

Only the radio static interference
of a sodium vapor light
illuminates a pack of neighborhood dogs
on an otherwise empty street

as they congregate around the corpse
of a half-eaten opossum,
its leathery red insides exposed,
like the outside of a deflated balloon,
its entrails scattered like bloody socks.

The leader bares its teeth and snarls
as I stumble onto the scene,
the others nervously awaiting a signal
invisible to me.

Just so the civilized world is wild
with this fear of its emptiness:

the quiet lights floating
on the face of the midnight stream;
the susurring nocturne chorus
perfecting its insanity.

The Invitation

  (after Carl Dennis)

I have an old invitation
serving as a bookmark between
pages 24 and 25 in my used copy of
The Modern Student's Library Edition
of *Matthew Arnold: Prose and Poetry*,
Copyright 1927, published by Scribner & Sons.
The book, according to a bookplate
about the size of a small return address label,
or a piece of tape, formerly belonged
to Willard B. Rockwood of 234 McKinley Street,
Minoa, New York. I bought it for
$1.50 at Carlson Turner Books
at 241 Congress Street in Portland's East End.
The invitation/bookmark is made of a stiff composite paper
and slightly larger and more square than a calling card,
yellowed almost to brown and spotted with age
so that it looks burned at the edges,
the strangely formal language
reading in printed gothic script:
"Please present this card at Franklin Hall,
Friday, November 21, 10 p.m., Mr. Pond."
Although the ink is faded, the polite command still hangs there:
an "invitation," from the Latin, *invitare*, to join life, in a way.
Mr. Pond, however, chose not to attend.
Perhaps he was one of those young men who
"hesitate and falter chance away,"
or perhaps, distracted by some sudden circumstance,
he was unforeseeably delayed and therefore missed his chance.
Perhaps there had been someone waiting for him
at Franklin Hall at 10 p.m., an acquaintance,
who was hoping to become something more, a friend,
and who was disappointed that Mr. Pond did not arrive.

I imagine Pond himself as a late-nineteenth-century striver,
marching forward under the gaslights of Willimantic.
Or I see him hailing a horse-drawn taxi if late,
slightly nervous of disposition, this young man,
old money, but new to Connecticut society, a bachelor, perhaps,
just establishing his rooms, keen on cultural events
of the sort that would be held at Franklin Hall,
lectures by great men of the time
or concerts of classical music, but also
ambivalent, unsure of himself and the demands
put on his social skills by intermission chatter
and the attentions of the opposite sex,
the kind of person who would accept such an invitation
but not attend. Much as I am
the sort of person to pick up the collected works
of Matthew Arnold, with every intention
to soldier obediently through, but then lose interest,
and, before I have made it past the opening essay,
forget why it had seemed important.
The bottom of the antique card marks
the place where I stopped reading
The Function of Criticism, where Arnold states:
"It is the business of the critical power, as I said
in the words already quoted, 'in all branches of knowledge,
theology, philosophy, history, art, science,
to see the object as in itself it really is.' Thus
it tends, at last, to make an intellectual situation
of which the creative power can profitably avail itself.
It tends to establish an order of ideas, if not absolutely true,
yet true by comparison with that which it displaces;
to make the best ideas prevail."

So like Arnold, so steadfast and Victorian
in his schoolmaster belief of one idea besting another,
and yet, in the phrase, "if not absolutely true,"
a hesitation, as if even he could sense the approach
of relativity and ambivalence just around the bend,
a world in which carefully treasured artifacts that had survived
centuries were doomed to be replaced by the latest new-fangled gadgets.
The card did not come with the book, but I found it
inside a family heirloom, an old traveling secretary,
sometimes called a lap desk, a wooden box,
hinged in the back, with a rich purple felt covering
both inside halves, these held fast with hook latches.
The woods, maple and pine, with a gold leaf design
painted on the top, now rubbed thin. Inside, under the felt writing pads,
an old ink bottle whose well has dried to a fragrant dust,
and ebony slim pens with brass nibs, the kind of writing instrument
almost like a scalpel that Matthew Arnold himself might have used
to carve his stern words on the thick-skinned page.
We had a lot of this kind of stuff hidden away in the house where I grew up.
The house itself was very modern, having been remodeled in the sixties
with plush wall-to-wall carpet in almost every room
and an attic the size of a small gymnasium, where
stacked on its plywood floors
were all sorts of family treasures we weren't supposed to touch,
and which, of course, we couldn't help explore:
the old revolutionary flintlock, my dad's
doctor bag from the fifties
when he was a resident at Philadelphia General,
inside of which was a dried-up vial of iodine,
not unlike the inkwell in the desk,
and a family bible, where the first birth in America was inscribed,
"Elizabeth Bacon, Salem 1647," who, it turns out,
would eventually marry someone named Pond,

the great-great-grandfather of the man who saved
the invitation I was now using as a bookmark.
Somehow all this got lost along the way:
my older brother sold the bible on eBay,
the flintlock, together with a spinning wheel,
ended up in a museum. Our family heritage
just wasn't an important part of our fondue-and-swim-meet lives;
we had fun, we played Kick the Can in the street
or tackle football in the yard.
Even our pretensions were thoroughly modern:
a French poodle, a Waterpik, and German cars.
Our house may have been the only house on the block
that had a "library," two bookshelves
flanking the fireplace in the living room,
where my parents would stack the books
they received from the book clubs to which they belonged,
modern editions of classics whose spines were rarely cracked,
The Sun Also Rises, *Travels With My Aunt*, *Darkness at Noon*,
and *The Last of the Mohicans*, but any knowledge
they contained was mostly ornamental—
the books themselves merely visible signs
of an old-fashioned, dying, country-club world where
my parents sent us all to private schools as soon as they could,
and, worse, made us all take dancing lessons,
interminable evenings wearing dark wool suits
and white cotton gloves, learning the steps
to the Foxtrot and the Waltz, while maintaining
a respectful distance between ourselves and the girls
who were taller and already knew the steps.
The climax of all this effort was the Cotillion
held each year in the ballroom of the Statler Hotel.

I remember receiving my own invitation in the mail,
its fine card stock and expensive calligraphy
like a death certificate in my hands,
"Mr. _____, you are cordially invited to attend."
I remember how I set the invitation down on the kitchen table,
went out back on the concrete deck to be alone,
forgetting a coat even though it was winter still, and not warm,
and with my hands wedged into my pockets,
stood and stared across the dark greasy fingers of the yard
at yesterday's snowfall patches crossed with pale yellow and gray
shadows of artificial light and felt the way
I often still feel when standing at the edge of something unfathomable—
that it is important that we not understand too much,
that one can be initiated into a conspiracy
without a single word being exchanged,
that this immensity can't help but rise above its limits,
overflow, and overtake us with its callous trajectory.

Sideshow

The interior of the house was drained of all color,
its greens and browns faded into a muted jaundice,
and between the Goodwill furniture were stacked
various things and parts of things
that had not yet been put out onto the street:
cases and cases of empty beer bottles,
aging newspapers and unfinished home repair projects,
like the desktop radio with its skyline insides exposed.
We used to listen to that radio all night long,
listen for the familiar pop songs turned up high,
so that we could not hear the dull shuffling of feet
and the inevitable refrain of escalating fights.
Once, after we had been warned
not to interfere with our older teenage sister,
who had an important date, we snuck out of bed,
and dragged two table chairs across the dirty floor,
so that we could stand on them and spy through the transom
into her bedroom and watch her boredom coalesce
as she tolerated the exertions of the clumsy stranger
who pressed her into her sagging mattress,
careful not to be discovered, despite our own dismay.
Yet in the dissatisfaction of the early morning light,
when all the displaced furniture and dirty glasses had been put away,
our sister laughed as we sang for her the song that we had heard,
after we had retreated from her humiliation and gone back to bed:
"Yummy, Yummy, Yummy, I got love in my tummy."
"Sing that again," she smiled. "That's a good one," she said.

The Last Poem I'll Ever Write

Every time I write a poem I'm sure
that it's the last, but then
I wander down an ordinary street
and look around
and see the strangeness of the narrow doors
and curtains drawn, the floating sound of music
from an upper room snowing down,
a dog who wanders out from in between
two buildings, all old familiars
of my nervous disposition,
all full of everything and empty too,
and there's really not much else
that I know how to do.

The Abandoned Psychiatric Hospital

What is it that is left behind
to remind us of what occupied this place?
Cracked plaster, broken glass, and peeling paint,
a colorless industrial gray mottled
by grime, mold, moisture, and decay,
so that there is no sign, no trace
of order sanitarily imposed
on the once defiant exiles of the human race.
The rubble of a roof caved in by its own sodden weight,
and a quiet and an emptiness large enough to contain
the numberless incommensurable souls.
No matter what complaints or wretched laughter
used to resound within these semi-solid walls,
no matter what singular thoughts used to echo
within the chambers of the inmates' brains,
at the end of a life of secrets it is the silence that remains,
and shafts of stale penetrating light that expose
a discarded mop handle and a piece of garden hose.

The Final Push

The agave blossoms only once and then it dies,
this one having waited more than seventy-five years
after being transplanted from the Amazon basin
to the arboretum at the University of Michigan,
shooting its totemic spike so high and fast—
six and one half inches every day—
that workers had to remove a panel of the greenhouse glass,
so that the bloom might tremble in the blue Ann Arbor sky
like a brightly painted avocado, gaudy and ridiculous,
while far below at the base of the ancient plant,
its leaves had already started to wrinkle and gray,
as would the face of an old woman lying in her bed at hospice,
who has just enough strength to lift her hand
and wave everything to be left behind away.

Close Enough

Sinatra sang "Witchcraft" in the background,
casting a magic spell.
You were the one to hum along
although we both knew the song pretty well.
We sat shoulder to shoulder,
like two lovers crowded into a photo booth,
only now the album of our youth was spread across our knees
as we browsed through snapshots taken long ago:
There I was hanging from a tree,
a confetti of leaves stuck to my tattered sweater,
the delicate haze of two days without shaving
spread wide by my grinning chin.
And you, your hands thrust in
and stretching the pockets of a borrowed coat,
your hair a whirlwind of pleasures.
You lingered as if to recall
a thought that would have gripped you then,
how already we together were older than original sin
and did not need to win from each other
what we were to fight for all our lives
and lose from each other over and over again.
And if I had reached out then to touch your hair,
once lustrous but now stiff and a little gray,
perhaps you would have been startled,
perhaps you would have relented;
but better to let pass this moment between us,
a moment close enough to sex,
let the dark catastrophe of our constant longing
remain an unspoken trust,
and not ruin a lifelong intimacy
with the stale breath of a scavenger lust.

The Angels at the Party

Their wings made it hard for them to squeeze through the door.
They had to humble themselves like animals at a zoo,
their downcast eyes still betraying their wildness,
although subdued by the embarrassment
of side-stepping strangers in confined spaces.
Each had to limit herself to a canapé or two.
They sampled the punch, laughed out loud
at jokes that really weren't that funny,
as if they didn't understand a thing being said.
One got too drunk and had to be carried out by the rest.
She was crying and shouting over her shoulder,
"You are all angels! You are all eternally blessed!"
So that, after they departed, it took a while for the party
to settle back into its normal patter.

Lucky Strikes

Back when we were intelligent
we all chain-smoked Lucky Strikes.
Cigarettes were our handheld devices.
Even Marcie, who was Canadian smart,
would light a smoke and take a drag
before she would launch into an intellectual tirade.
Remember her tall red-headed boyfriend from Montreal?
He was more serious than anyone we knew.
He could say with a straight face
that he belonged to this or that philosophical school.
All the boys wore tight-fitting thrift-store suits
and piles of hair in front so that
they could brush it back from their eyes.
The girls for their part wore vintage dresses and shoes.
We stayed up all night,
dancing to old Motown and The B-52s
until we were so exhausted or so drunk
that we could hardly stand,
dehydrated from speed, coke, and booze.
The ones who couldn't sleep would migrate to the derelict park
where the early dawn had not yet risen over the hill
and where the rats had their nests
among the rotted pilings at the dark water's edge.
Not far from the abandoned basketball courts,
the backboards hung like empty signs on iron poles,
we found a bench with only two slats missing,
a few dispirited pigeons milling about our feet,
hoping that we might spill something.
Each of us lit another cigarette, the small fires
like two dust-filled fuses sizzling,
to cultivate and chase away that feeling of being alone
even when you're sitting next to your friend,
staring out across the river at nothing in particular.

At the Pompeii Gift Shop

You can buy a t-shirt that says
Omnia Vincit Amor,
which is ironic because
it is not at all clear
from the exhibit
that this is true:
among the mummified remains
of small children
and disconsolate slaves
is a petrified couple
who embrace,
the man
trying to shield
his lover's face
from the rain
of ash and stone
about to fuse them
into what will be
their place in history,
his last words,
if she heard them at all,
permanently
erased.

La Chevy Nova

When in the middle of my life
I park my car at the edge of the city woods,
the rain tapping its smog-stained fingers
on the dirty hood of my twenty-year-old Chevrolet,
I let the engine idle while Nat King Cole
sings "Hit That Jive, Jack" from 1941.
And my mind wanders to thoughts of my grandfather,
whom I never met, although he, like me,
was a jazz drummer, a classicist, and a writer of poetry.
He found an ideal home in between-the-wars Berlin,
perhaps because he was a racist and adulterer,
who swore at other drivers, calling them "dirty Catholics."
He died in Teaneck when he was fifty-five of a heart attack,
the result of too much everything, discovered
frozen at the wheel of his old Chevy outside his mistress' den,
just as I sit, listening to the jumping bebop of the radio broadcast,
wondering if the rain, like a ghostly grace,
will wash away my ancestral sins,
until I find myself snapping my fingers in time
to the rockin' rhythm, just grateful enough, just, to be alive.

The Longest Day of the Year

It had taken us three to four hours—I can never really tell—
what with gas stops and snack stops and just pulling to the side of the road,
to drive to Mount Desert, then three or four more to drive back,
all to spend two nights sleeping on a hotel bed,
one day brilliant white and blue and sitting by the pool,
the next day all gray with the cold damp dripping from the trees,
and we imprisoned in our room with the TV drooling on,
the books we meant to read propped up on our knees.
We wanted to get back in time to go to Teresa's party,
a garden potluck, where everyone was supposed to bring a rock
to contribute to the little Zen Stonehenge she had patiently created.
I had one saved from a recent walk on the beach,
the dullest and most ordinary one I could find,
because I am tired of trying to compete, of trying to present
the most unusual, the most breathtaking, or most significant stone.
But by the time we got home, we were too exhausted to attend,
and so pulled together some leftovers from the fridge,
fed the chickens and the cat, gave our daughter a bath,
and then before the long summer twilight had turned itself to dusk,
I took the rock outside and threw it as far as I could
into the deep and shadow-woven woods and listened
for the satisfying sound of an ordinary stone
crashing through the branches and finally hitting the ground.

Superman

We used to fly down hills
in the grip of our own velocity,
the frames of our bikes shaking in our hands,
our feet tripping over each other faster than we could run.

There was no harm in falling—it was part of the fun.
Our parents weren't around to scold us.
And when they were, they didn't care.
There was, after all, "revolution in the air."

The grown-ups mixed cocktails, played bridge, were late getting home from work.
Like stubborn oracles, they appeared mostly on holidays,
when everything was arranged so that they could present us
with the toys and games we craved, without too much fuss.

There's a picture of me standing before the Christmas tree,
which is three times as tall as I will ever be
and draped in lights, beads, and glass ornaments,
like a green-limbed, many-armed dowager aunt,
propped up in the corner for the occasion.
I am wearing the outfit of Superman,
too big for my shoulders, its baggy folds
cinched around my waist with a bathrobe pull,
my hands on my hips in a suitable superhero pose,
invincible, even in my Clark Kent glasses,
the empty box at my feet,
like a hamlet I have just rescued from destruction.

McDonald's Lobster Roll

"Is nothing sacred?" my father would joke,
a man who was an atheist all his life.
In 1935, when he was 12, his parents tied him to his bed
because he was, in the vernacular of the day, a raving lunatic,
and they couldn't afford to pay the bill collectors
who haunted his childhood home, (my Grandpa Ed
jumping over the backyard fence to evade them)
much less a round of adolescent hospitalization.
Years later my father explained that his nervous breakdown
was the result of an existential question. At the age of 12,
he couldn't comprehend how life had any meaning.
So, wrists and ankles shackled by corded sheets,
he thrashed about in spiritual despair
until an unfamiliar voice came into his head
and suggested, "What if there is no God?"
It was this non-belief that saved him.
And yet also condemned him to a jocular irony
that cleared the way for just this sort of fast-food atrocity,
which would have offended someone of more conviction.
But neither of us seemed to mind as we savored
the sweet and fatty meat, the sugared and caffeinated drink,
and the fries like candied treats, each part
of the *corpus delicti*.

A Depressed Man Experiences Joy

I saw the future today smoking a pipe,
riding a bicycle and smoking a pipe,
pedaling backwards as she sailed down the hill,
hair flying behind her like a fusillade of ribbons,
or the tattered tail of a kite, her hands on the handlebars,
the corncob pipe clenched between her teeth
in a grimace of delight as she sailed down the hill
into the future, smoking her pipe, on her candy-colored bike,
clicking her little bell to warn slowpokes to scatter,
her tattersall basket filled to the brim
with groceries, and, well, I thought the future
was beautiful and free and basically inaccessible
to me.

The Ballerina on the Golden Bicycle

A Hollywood starlet introduces her,
a starlet just past the decades of her fame,
Joan Crawford in a green dress,
a satiny green cocktail dress
so elaborate and sensuous
that, when she moves,
it is like the whispering
of a harem slave by whom
she is nonchalantly possessed.
She does a professional job of pronouncing
the difficult, foreign-sounding name,
Lilly Yokoi, to the audience which we cannot see.
We, the television audience,
also sit outside the camera's rigid frame,
as if the television in the living room
were no more than a miniature stage,
the medium still rooted
in the theatre or the circus,
and the variety show hosted by Ms. Crawford
the last incarnation
of a dying vaudeville tradition
from a time when people were still amazed
by the exertions of other people
who worked years to perfect a skill
to entertain them: in this case,
a middle-aged Japanese-American woman
on a gold-plated, customized bike,
whose balance and command
of the wheeled vehicle
is so poised and astute
that she can do a handstand
on the handlebars
while the back wheel
pirouettes behind her,

the moment in the show,
which Ms. Crawford announces in a voice-over,
is the most difficult trick she knows,
navigating through the condescending applause
of the Vietnam-era middle-class whites,
who have come all the way to Hollywood
to see the exotic sights.

The Stuff That Flies Around

Every day is an emergency, otherwise
not much to say, rice paper leaves
crackling with light, the trees
dripping and dying with the autumn light.
(There is no way to get it right.)
Small brown birds dart in and out
of the branches that shake the flaming leaves,
like fighter pilots on a lark.
My quizzical next-door neighbor,
with her hands on her hips, the prelude
to a question burning on her lipsticked lips,
asks, "Where do they all come from?
I don't see a nest," while squirrels nervously
tack from wire to branch to wire and back.

Decomposing Nicely

Some colors one can only see
when overcast with shadow,
the late fall-rusted trees,
red clay and rock outcropping,
winter light now faded yellow
on dead grass and the meadow marsh,
how it clings to the poisoned leaves,
all phosphorescent with decline,
all dragged beside the window of the train,
the closest things so fleeting,
the distant stilled by threat of rain,
obscured by chiaroscuros of dying light,
not as a world on fire
but fixed by bloodstains of the sun,
pooled in a landscape given sway and hum
by the rocking of the carriage,
all decomposing nicely,
each whispering an open secret:
that beauty ruins everything,
draws to itself all quiet sense
and all crepuscular thought,
only to paint the gloam of lust
with some romantic desperate hope.

Dante Gabriel Rosetti to Elizabeth

I have entombed my love poems to you
in the moldering casket of your heart.
Yet I keep returning to the plot of grass,
keep mumbling the half-forgotten phrases out loud,
haunted by visions of decomposition,
like an evening sky of purpling clouds.
As the flesh creeps back from the sockets around your eyes,
your soft hair dries into angel-hair kindling,
and your wedding ring loosens on your bony finger.
After seven years I cannot take it any longer
and break every solemn vow I have ever made,
hire common laborers to dig through the soft dirt to your grave,
casting aside all sentiment, sweating with nervous pride,
to steal once again what you treasured best,
the manuscript of my devotion from your lifeless breast.

The Former Slaughterhouse at Villa Epecuén

Among a stand of long dead trees
bleached white by the intense salinity
of flood waters that consumed the town,
a road built in the seventies still winds around
the former slaughterhouse at Villa Epecuén.
For twenty-five years local fish and eels have passed
through windows filled with shadow now instead of glass
and around the abandoned art deco tower
and the enormous block letters spelling *Matadero*.
But now the scabrous edifice sits alone,
its plaster surfaces peeling and its facade collapsed,
like a skin-diseased bather come to take the cure,
who, waiting by the roadside, isn't sure
whether she has missed the last bus back to Carhué.

House of Cards

Each time I look outside, the rain, invisible and mute,
erases more and more of the dwindling day.
My mother rhythmically shuffles the well-worn cards,
an expert at manipulating the deck,
the sound she makes like the unzipping of a cloth valise
in which she has stored her simple tricks.
"The game is rummy," she announces with a condescending smile,
before she deals me my ten cards
and sets the deck between us like a tiny house
with its many doors, each opening to a dull surprise
of domestic disappointment or delight.
But there is no mystery about who will prevail.
My mother is master of both the game and me.
What matters is the leisured clocking of this borrowed time,
and her ardent concentration on both the game and me,
as close to each other as we will ever get.

The Unbearable Lightness of Being Fifteen

As I was marching up a narrow mountain path,
an ascent so rocky it was almost a scree—
my breaths struggling to keep pace with my heartbeat,
the sweat soaking into the band of my baseball cap—
I heard laughter caroling down the stony channel.
And when we collided—the two young lovers and I—
their eyes bright with the fun of reckless steps bouncing along
the same trail which I now methodically climbed,
I clambered onto the back of a bordering rock to let them pass.
There is nothing more important in the world
than two fifteen-year-olds laughing and holding hands,
perfecting again the awkward art of skipping together
headlong and carefree down a treacherous slope.

On Looking for my Friend and Not Finding Him

It was a whim to leave the interstate,
taking MA 128 to the nearby town,
not inspired by any nostalgic vanity
but just to see if my friend, Jeffrey Harrison, was around.
Centre Street wound through unfamiliar wooded country,
so I couldn't safely use my phone
and wasn't sure he'd be home when I arrived.
I found the house all right.
There was a brand new Honda parked in the drive.
But the dog didn't bark as I walked around back,
which wasn't a good sign.
Nobody answered when I pulled the screen door open
and knocked on one of the little panes,
the 19th-century farmhouse as quiet as the light rain
which had begun to fall on the tire swing in the yard,
abandoned long ago by his children grown tall and gone to college.
In the part of the kitchen I could see,
there was an empty glass—its insides coated
by a milky film—and a plate on the counter next to it,
where perhaps a sandwich had once been.
Every time I visit Jeff makes me a sandwich!
I scanned the nearby woods,
the woods that feature so often in his poems,
a landscape mostly deserted by his neighbors with jobs in town,
the trees as lonely as trees could be,
except for a crow planted on a crooked telephone pole,
who cocked his head and cawed at me,
then puffed his wings as if to say,
"Get out of here—You're trespassing."

Loggerheads

Because my light was brighter, you let me go ahead
on the scrub path through stinging sea grass to the beach.
This was in prehistoric times when teenagers wore
flat-bottomed sneakers and tight-fitting straight-legged jeans,
just before developers built a rampart of condominiums
along the constantly collecting and constantly dissolving shore.
I forget how it was we knew
that tonight was the night that the earth was sure to move.
But we set the alarm, coaxed each other out of bed,
and stumbled forward toward the sound of dark surf rolling back and forth.
You were the first to see, and you grabbed me from behind
to keep my step from trespassing on what was an ancient rite:
the almost imperceptible sight of strong-willed monsters as they rose and fell,
each carapace laboring up the strand to mate and bury its nest,
as if the beach itself were breathing in and out
in patient silent duty, as if all nature
had the same anxious premonition, as if our being there was a sign,
and my stupidly shining my flashlight into the reptile eyes
a match to set the tropical world ablaze.

Grace

The vanes of the radiometer
rotate when fanned by light,
not unlike the leaves of a trembling ash
on the first warm day of spring
or the bristles of a paintbrush,
which the careful girl wets with her tongue
to bring it to a finer point
before her delicate application
of radioactive paint
to the military watch face
at United States Radium.
When the ghost whistle blows,
Grace and the other girls
spill onto the orange streets,
like charged particles
emanating from a core,
an ionized feminine vapor dissipating
into the early evening's medium.
Between the gossip of the factory
and the indeterminacies of life,
each girl has a private world to explore:
uncertain crushes, family squabbles,
and numerous mundane chores,
while all the while the isotope
spreads from the ungular base to the chin,
wreaking its necrotic alchemy,
turning iron into water
and bones brittle and thin.

Bright Star

I can't believe how feeble you are,
Venus, in the early morning eastern sky,
flickering like the single engine light of a distant boat
floating on a trash-strewn sea
or the blinking eye of an insomniac satellite
aimlessly spying on me.
No matter how far you have drifted
or from what alien time-worn shore,
I cannot track your progress—
you seem hopelessly stuck in place—
a hole in the fabric of the darkness
through which we perceive too late
the dying flame of an antique world until
the color drains from dawn's cloud-blemished face,
and you disappear into the crowded day,
like something or someone forgotten.

Music Unheard

I like the guy
pacing around in the background,
listening and chatting on his cell phone,
whom the viewer can see
through the storefront window
of a Marin County eatery,
where Kay Ryan sits,
explaining why she writes such short poems
(in fact, if this were one of her own,
it would end about here)
and how each poem she writes
is a kind of sass,
backtalk to something she heard or read.
Then there's the guy who's a ringer for my dead brother,
stomping through the Central Park Zoo,
like a large angry ape escaped from his cage,
not looking at anything,
not even the camera,
while Kay talks in a voice-over
about her poem "How Birds Sing,"
which is on display on a plaque nearby.
We don't know what the one guy is saying
and don't know why the other is so enraged.
But there they are, you can't ignore them:
both inadvertent prisoners
of this documentary about poetry.
And they will always distract me
from whatever point the film is making.

The Riptide

I am neither young nor old.
Plenty of my friends have died.
Some were thoughtless suicides.

Most were overdosed.
Although there were one or two
whom disease caught by surprise.

I am more cold than warm
as I stand against the wind
and stare out at the ocean,

where the titanic currents jostle
against the world that holds them close.
A submarine shelf makes the giant water stand

witness to its own dissolution,
briny sinews corded together
unravelling on the beach,

like a furious hand
clawing at the sand
which it cannot hold.

I hope my family has pity on me
as I dive into the Atlantic
and swim out past the swell,

where the waves that will break
upon the strand are mounting.
I enjoy the way the ocean lifts me up

but does not release me into the air,
confident that I'll be all right
until I lose sight of the land.

The Eclogues

I was reading the *Eclogues* of Virgil
while sitting on a broken toilet seat
in the graffiti-smeared bathroom of CBGB's
not twenty feet downstairs from the back door,
which opened onto a dumpster where once I discovered
the dead body of a naked teenage girl.
She was one of the indistinguishable runaways
from some who-knows-where hick town,
who used to haunt the club, begging change.
At first I thought she was a mannequin
or an incredibly lifelike sex doll
someone had thrown over the razor-topped fence,
her eyes frozen open, her legs splayed,
her skin unspoiled.
She was blond like a famous rock singer
and her hair had been cut in the same way,
straight bangs across her eyebrows.
People used to claim that prostitutes
gave blowjobs in the stall where I was reading,
servicing johns to pay for heroin habits,
a spot no more sordid than the average cubicle
where Roman prostitutes would ply their trade,
a city so filthy and teeming with vice
that Virgil, like his Hellenistic predecessors,
composed bucolic poetry as an idealized antidote
to the daily degradations of urban life,
where apartment dwellers would routinely empty pots of shit
on the heads of pedestrians five stories below.
The girl I found didn't have any obvious track marks,
and the police wouldn't tell us how she died.
No matter; it was her idyllic fantasies that killed her,
thinking she could escape to a place better than where she was,
just as I might think that reading Latin poetry
would transport me from my surroundings.

The ambulance turned its searchlight off
as it ferried her away to the morgue.
She would never find whatever it was she was looking for
in the broken glass and garbage-filled lot behind the club.
Instead her uncomprehending parents would have to drive
to New York to identify her and make arrangements
to have what was left of her shipped home.
All to pour her ashes into some polluted and feeble stream
where once had been her favorite chestnut tree,
but where now not much green would grow.

Walking Through my Hometown Just Before Winter

In late November the afternoons are dark,
the streets deserted but for a few anxious cars,
which crawl around under the ghoulish lights,
the sky as gray as if there were no stars,
the sky a fathomless monotonous decay
into which the bare-tree broken limbs
reach for the invisible stars, but find instead
only the flakes of a gentle fragmentation,
the first snow like the world falling apart,
the fugitive leaves huddled near the drains,
and the normal trespassers of the hour all wending home
because there is no light beyond this tarnished day.

Ubi Mater Est

Where is my mother now
with her nervous stomach,
her short-cropped steel-wool hair,
her blue eyes like cough drops,
and her trembling hands
lighting one cigarette on another?
Misery was her lollipop
as she undid the crossword puzzle in pen
and left us drunkenly scrawled notes
which we couldn't comprehend.
She would take her false teeth out,
put them on the table beside her bed,
and sleep until the afternoon,
drifting through the house like a fabled ghost
that just wanted to retrieve its head.
We burned her corpse in a cardboard box,
scattered her ashes in a blustering wind,
so that they flew back in our faces,
dandruff on the shoulders of our funeral clothes;
she clings to me still, that ancient curse,
or worse, the flame she was consumed in,
burning darkly on the brightest snow-dazzled day,
loose flakes shaking from the tree limbs.

The Normal Rhythmic Clenching of the Heart

As when a boy climbs onto the railing of a bridge
which connects two tottering walls of granite face
so tall the furious waterfall below which furrowed the ancient gorge
cannot be heard. But like an optical illusion
that seems to crawl when everything else is still
or a phosphorescent reflection etched on windshield glass,
it hypnotizes the perilous child, who feels the wind
I cannot feel, as if he were a ragged flag.
He's not afraid to sit atop the balustrade
and intertwine his sneakers in the rusted posts,
when, like a sudden forgetting, his paper kite
escapes his grasp and spirals into its private destiny,
a vertiginous beckoning whirlpool, a panicked diastole.

The Old Man in the Mirror

The best poem is no poem, no music, nothing,
radio off, driving through the driving snow,
everything almost invisible,
like driving through a swarm
of dying wishes.

There is an old man behind me,
his arms and his chin hung
over the wheel of his car,
his eyes like two headlights
dimmed by the furious snow.

He won't get off my tail,
as if he were afraid of something behind us,
something pushing us forward and pursuing us at the same time,
and, in fact, my own eyes keep straying to the rearview mirror,
but there is nothing, just the old man and the driving snow.

Keith Dunlap graduated in 1987 from Columbia College with a BA in English, where he studied poetry with Kenneth Koch and David Shapiro. He received his MPhil in Classical Literature and Philology from Columbia University in 1992. He is a former co-editor of *The Columbia Review* and a former co-editor of *Cutbank*, the literary magazine of the graduate program in creative writing at the University of Montana, where he received his MFA IN 2000. In the eighties and nineties, Mr. Dunlap played drums and percussion in several bands in NYC and was a repertory member of the avant-garde theatre company, The New York Art Theatre Institute. His poetry has appeared in numerous journals.

www.ingramcontent.com/pod-product-compliance
Lightning Source LLC
Chambersburg PA
CBHW070208100426
42743CB00013B/3091